RAGTIME JUBILEE

42 Piano Gems, 1911–21

Edited by
DAVID A. JASEN

DOVER PUBLICATIONS, INC.
Mineola, New York

Bibliographical Note

Ragtime Jubilee: 42 Piano Gems, 1911–21 is a new collection of sheet music with original covers, selected and with an introduction by David A. Jasen, first published by Dover Publications, Inc., in 1997. The original publishers and dates of publication of the music appear in the Contents and on the individual covers and title pages.

International Standard Book Number: 0-486-29946-5

Manufactured in the United States of America
Dover Publications, Inc., 31 East 2nd Street, Mineola, N.Y. 11501

INTRODUCTION

The decade 1911–1921 was the booming adolescence of ragtime. A dozen or so years had now passed since the first ragtime publications, and this ear-catching, toe-tapping piano style was gradually coming into its full flowering.

Driving this evolution was the increasing interest of a new breed of composer-pianists—busy pros who had filled a hungry piano-roll industry with countless arrangements of popular songs. Here were such stars as Charley Straight, Max Kortlander, Lee S. Roberts, Felix Arndt, Roy Bargy and the prolific Zez Confrey. Their involvement refreshed old ragtime forms and contents. The technical level of pieces—formerly written for the average pianist—was now raised to new levels as the composer-pianist designed the music as a piano-roll showcase for his own keyboard talents.

Rhythmic clichés of traditional ragtime—especially the overused three-over-four pattern—were gradually dropped in favor of more inventive, more complex patterns and textures. Harmonies became richer and keyboard "stylings" became the rage of the years after World War I.

In this heady time, with everyone wanting to get into the act, old pros—the stars of ragtime's first decade—continued with their happy melodies as veterans like Charles L. Johnson, Henry Lodge, Percy Wenrich, Harry Tierney and George Botsford joined talented newcomers Charles L. Cooke, Jack Glogau, Fred Heltman, Nat Johnson, Paul Pratt, George L. Cobb, Lew Pollack and Carleton Colby.

As early as 1913–14, Julius Lenzberg—the most significant ragtime composer of the teens—made his mark ragging the classics, notably with "Hungarian Rag" and "Operatic Rag" (quoting from both Franz Liszt and *Carmen*)—certainly an influence on George L. Cobb's hit of 1918, the million-selling "Russian Rag" . . . *"interpolating the world-famous 'Prelude' by Rachmaninoff."*

By the late teens, "novelty" rags—an evolutionary step that would bloom fully in publications of the 1920's—began to appear on piano rolls. Here was the impact of a white, European, classical tradition on a form born in rural black America. Ragtime syncopations mixed with classical harmonies, elements of French impressionism (Ravel and Debussy were hot items of those years), and such piano-roll devices as "breaks" (decorative, cascading runs down the keyboard) and melodies played in harmonic intervals of thirds and fourths. With their idiomatic triplets and dotted rhythms, Roy Bargy's "Blue Streak" and "Rufenreddy" (written with Charley Straight), and Zez Confrey's "My Pet" are perfect examples of the form. All three appeared on rolls many months before their sheet-music publication.

A much-delayed fate played on other rags of the 1911-1921 decade. Henry Kleinkauf and Guy Hall waited thirty-three years—and the recording by Russ Morgan's orchestra—for "Johnson Rag" to reach hit-parade status. Other rags waited longer still, reaching popularity only in ragtime's first great revival, in the 1950's.

Immediate hit or patient plodder, there is much here for all of us pianists: the abundance of an engaging slice of popular keyboard repertory in all of its delightful, toe-tapping riches . . . the many faces of ragtime in its most inventive decade of far-reaching change.

David A. Jasen

CONTENTS

THE AEROPLANE
RAG AND TWO-STEP
by
JACK GLOGAU
Composer of "KING SOL" March, "GOLDEN KNIGHT" March, "THE PACE THAT KILLS" ETC.
WILL ROSSITER THE CHICAGO PUBLISHER
136 W. LAKE ST, CHICAGO, ILL.
ALBERT & SON SYDNEY AUSTRALIA.
COPYRIGHT MCMXII BY WILL ROSSITER
5
PUBLISHED FOR BAND AND ORCHESTRA

THE AEROPLANE
(RAG and TWO-STEP).

JACK GLOGAU.

Tempo Rag (*not too fast*)

Copyright MCMXIII Will Rossiter. Chicago, Ill.

4   *The Aeroplane*

ANGEL FOOD

(RAG)

BY

Al Marzian

FORSTER MUSIC PUBLISHER
529 S. WABASH AVE. CHICAGO

5

"ANGEL FOOD"

(RAG)

A. F. MARZIAN.

Slowly.

Blame It On The Blues
A WEARY BLUE

CHAS. L. COOKE
Writer of
"Heroes Of The Balkans"
"Snappin' Turtle Rag"

Tempo di Ragioso

Blame It on the Blues

The Blue Grass Rag.
One Step.

By CHAS. STRAIGHT.

Piano.

J.M.Co. 607–3

BLUE MOON
(Fox Trot)
by
Lee S. Roberts
and
Max Kortlander
Pub. by Lee S. Roberts, Fine Arts Building, Chicago, Ill.

BLUE MOON

FOX - TROT

MAX KORTLANDER
and LEE S. ROBERTS

Moderato

Copyright, MCMXVIII, by Lee S. Roberts
410 Fine Arts Bldg., Chicago, Ill.

19

BLUE STREAK

DEDICATED TO
AND INTRODUCED BY
BENSON
OF CHICAGO

MAY BE HAD FOR
TALKING MACHINE
AND
PLAYER PIANO

BY
ROY BARGY
60

FORSTER
MUSIC PUBLISHER INC.
235 SOUTH WABASH AVE
CHICAGO

VAN DOORN MORGAN

Blue Streak

RAG FOX-TROT

By ROY BARGY

Very Slow

The BOUNDING BUCK

FOX TROT

COMPOSED BY

HENRY LODGE

WRITER OF
TEMPTATION RAG, MISERY BLUES,
HIFALUTIN RAG, IN THE SPOTLIGHT WALTZ.

50¢
2⁵/₌NET

M. WITMARK & SONS
NEW YORK CHICAGO PHILADELPHIA BOSTON SAN FRANCISCO LONDON

The Bounding Buck

A Rag Dance

By HENRY LODGE

Canadian Capers

N.B. The bass notes indicated thus: ♩ may be omitted and the bass board struck with the foot.

GUS   BERT   HENRY
CHANDLER - WHITE & COHEN

Copyright MCMXV by Roger Graham.
145 North Clark St.,   Chicago, Ill.

Clover Club
A
Fox Trot
Classic
by
Felix Arndt
60
RAY
Sam Fox Pub. Co.
Cleveland
EUROPEAN REPRESENTATIVES, BOSWORTH & CO. LONDON

CLOVER CLUB
A FOX TROT CLASSIC

FELIX ARNDT
Composer of "Nola" etc.

CRADLE ROCK

FOX-TROT

By
ABE FRANKL *and*
PHIL. KORNHEISER

POPULAR EDITION
LEO. FEIST INC. NEW YORK
ASCHERBERG, HOPWOOD & CREW. LDT. LONDON ENGLAND

5

Cradle-Rock

(FOX-TROT)

By ABE FRANKL
& PHIL. KORNHEISER

Allegro moderato

CRAZY BONE RAG

BY
CHAS. L. JOHNSON

FORSTER MUSIC PUBLISHER
529 S. WABASH AVE.
CHICAGO

CRAZY BONE RAG

CHAS. L. JOHNSON

TRIO

The Foot Warmer.

One-Step or Two-Step.

By HARRY PUCK.

Trio.

Fred Heltman's RAG

5

by

FRED HELTMAN

Published for
Orchestra

Fred Heltman Co. ⋎ ⋎ ⋎ Cleveland, Ohio.

FRED HELTMAN'S RAG

By FRED HELTMAN
Composer of "Chewin' The Rag"
"Shine or Polish Rag," etc.

Slow Rag

FRISCO FRAZZLE

BY
Nat Johnson

(F.J.A.)
FORSTER MUSIC PUBLISHER
529 S. WABASH AVE.
CHICAGO

5

'FRISCO FRAZZLE

RAG TWO-STEP

NAT JOHNSON

Moderato

Frisco Frazzle

Good-Bye Rag

A FOX-TROT

BY
CARLETON L. COLBY

PUBLISHED IN THE FOLLOWING ARRANGEMENTS

PianoSolo	.60
Orchestration - 11 & Pia.	.75
Orchestration - Full & Pia.	1.00
Band	.50

HAROLD ROSSITER MUSIC COMPANY
Chicago — 323-325 W. Madison St. — Illinois

GOOD-BYE RAG

By CARLETON L. COLBY.

Not too fast.

FEATURED IN VAUDEVILLE BY ALEXANDER AND BELDING
GOOD GRAVY
RAG
BY
HARRY BELDING
PUBLISHED BY
BUCK & LOWNEY
"PUBLISHERS OF MUSIC THAT SELLS"
ST. LOUIS, MO.

GOOD GRAVY RAG

(A MUSICAL RELISH)

By HARRY BELDING

"HAPPY RAG"

By R. G. GRADI

5

PUBLISHED BY
AJAX MUSIC CO.
CHICAGO · ILLINOIS

HAPPY RAG

RAGTIME ESSENCE

R. G. GRADY

Tempo di Rag

Copyright MCMXIII by Ajax Music Co.
Chicago, Ill.

HAREM SCAREM RAG

BY

LEM TROMBLEY

WRITER OF
"Story of A Rose," "The Truest Love"
"Why Don't You Smile," Etc.

5

PVBLISHED BY THE
GEO. L. TROMBLEY PUB. CO.,
KALAMAZOO, MICHIGAN.

"HAREM SCAREM RAG"

Moderato.

G. L. TROMBLEY.

HAUNTING RAG
INSTRUMENTAL
By
JULIUS LENZBERG
50¢
2/-
M. WITMARK & SONS
NEW YORK · CHICAGO · SAN FRANCISCO · LONDON · PARIS

Haunting Rag.

JULIUS LENZBERG.

Not too fast.

Hot-House Rag.

PAUL PRATT.

TRIO.

HUNGARIAN RAG

BY JULIUS LENZBERG

JEROME H. REMICK & CO. New York Detroit.

"Hungarian Rag"

By JULIUS LENZBERG
Composer of "Haunting Rag" etc.

Hyacinth Rag

By
George Botsford

HYACINTH

RAG

GEORGE BOTSFORD
Comp. of "Black and White" Rag

JOHNSON RAG
FOX TROT
By
Guy Hall
AND
Henry Kleinkauf

Hall's Banjo Orchestra.

FEATURED BY

Hall's Banjo Orchestra
WILKES-BARRE, PA.

PUBLISHED BY
HALL & KLEINKAUF
WILKES-BARRE, PA.

JOHNSON RAG
FOX TROT

HENRY KLEINKAUF
&
GUY HALL

Tempo di Drag

D. S. al Fine.

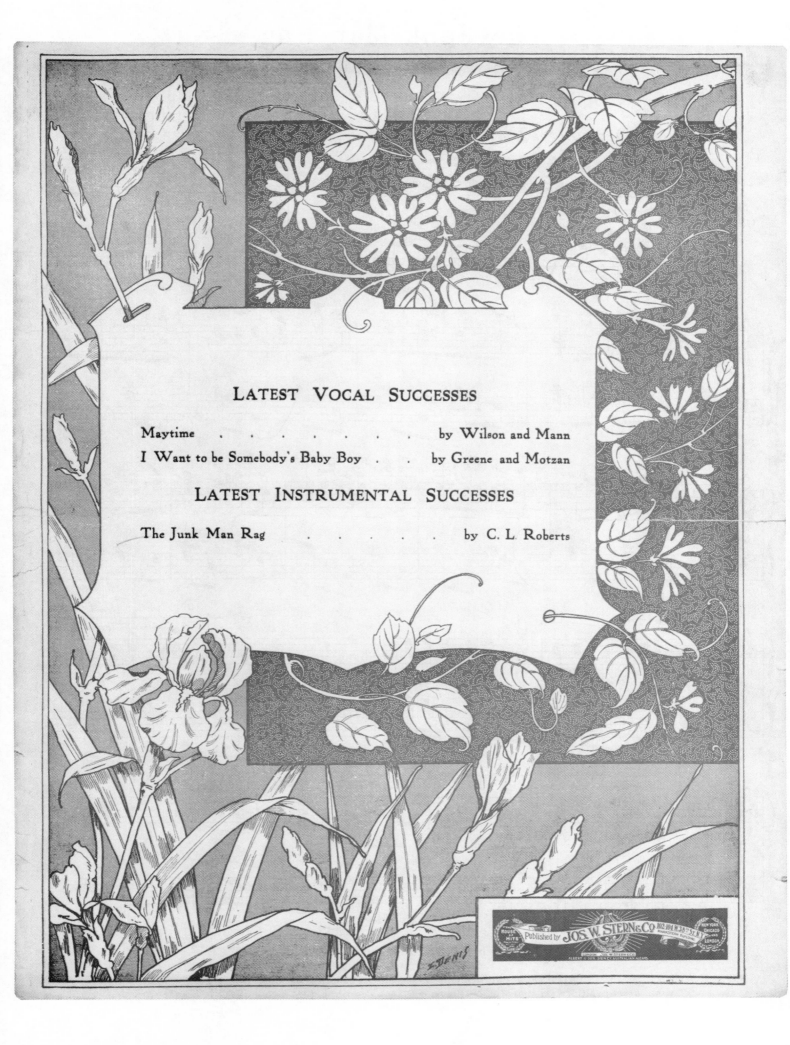

LATEST VOCAL SUCCESSES

Maytime . . . . by Wilson and Mann

I Want to be Somebody's Baby Boy . . . by Greene and Motzan

LATEST INSTRUMENTAL SUCCESSES

The Junk Man Rag . . . . . . by C. L. Roberts

Published by JOS. W. STERN & CO. 102-104 W. 38th ST. N.Y.

The Junk Man Rag

C. LUCKYTH ROBERTS.
(LUCKEY)
Arranged by Wm H. Tyers.

Les Copeland's
38th. STREET RAG.

By LES COPELAND

TRIO.

The MAZIE KING MIDNIGHT TROT

MAZIE KING and TED DONER

As Originally Introduced in America by

MAZIE KING

Written by

GEORGE L. COBB

Writer of "JUST FOR TO-NIGHT" ETC

ALSO PUBLISHED FOR BAND AND ORCHESTRA

5

WILL ROSSITER

THE CHICAGO PUBLISHER

136 W. LAKE ST. CHICAGO, ILL.

COPYRIGHT MCMXVI BY WILL ROSSITER

Starmer

MAZIE KING

The Midnight Trot

(A Novelty One Step and Trot)
(MAXIXE.)

GEORGE L. COBB
Composer of "Just For To-Night" etc

Allegro

The Midnight Trot

The Midnight Trot

MUSLIN RAG

Price Sixty Cents

BY
Mel. B. Kaufman

60

FORSTER MUSIC PUBLISHER INC. CHICAGO.

MUSLIN RAG
One Step

MEL.B.KAUFMAN

Trio

My Pet

—

ZEZ CONFREY'S
NOVELTY PIANO
SOLOS

AS PLAYED ON
PHONOGRAPH RECORDS and PIANO ROLLS
BY THE COMPOSER

KITTEN ON THE KEYS
MY PET
GREENWICH WITCH
POOR BUTTERMILK
YOU TELL 'EM, IVORIES

60 cents

Published by
JACK MILLS INC.
152-154 West 45th Street,
NEW YORK

My Pet

Allegro moderato

ZEZ CONFREY

staccato

Operatic Rag

By JULIUS LENZBERG
Composer of: "Hungarian Rag"

SOLO BASSI

Pork and Beans
One Step-Two Step or Turkey Trot.

By C. LUCKYTH ROBERTS.
Composer of "The Junk Man."

Pork and Beans

Rooster Rag

Roy Bargy
PIANO
SYNCOPATIONS
RUFENREDDY

1 Slipova   60 net
2 Justin-Tyme   .60
3 Sunshine Capers .60
4 Pianoflage   .60
5 Rufenreddy   .60
6 Knice and Knifty .60
7 Jim Jams   .60
8 Behave Yourself .60

SamFox Pub.Co.
CLEVELAND   NEW YORK
European Representatives Bosworth & Co. London

Rufenreddy

ROY BARGY
in collaboration with
CHARLEY STRAIGHT

Moderato

Russian Rag

by George L. Cobb

Interpolating the World Famous "Prelude" by Rachmaninoff

Originally Introduced on the American Stage
by Mlle. Rhea

Piano Solo 60 cents.
Small Orchestra and Piano acc. 75 cents.
Full Orchestra and Piano acc. $1.00.
Band (32 parts) 75 cents.

Published by
 WILL ROSSITER
THE CHICAGO PUBLISHER.
71 W. RANDOLPH STREET   CHICAGO, ILL.
Copyright MCMXVIII by WILL ROSSITER

RUSSIAN RAG

Interpolating the world famous,"PRELUDE," by Rachmaninoff

by GEORGE L. COBB

Moderato *Not too fast*

SOME JAZZ
FOX-TROT
BY
S. J. STOCCO
5
Jerome H. Remick & Co.,
DETROIT ~ NEW YORK

SOME JAZZ
FOX TROT

S. J. STOCCO

SPRING TIME ~RAG~

By
Paul Pratt

5

PUBLISHED BY JOHN STARK & SON, SAINT LOUIS.

Spring-time Rag.

PAUL PRATT.

INTRO.
Moderato

TEASING RAG

PAUL PRATT

That Madrid Rag

BY Julius Lenzberg

TED SNYDER Co.
MUSIC PUBLISHERS
112 WEST 38 St. NEW YORK.

5

THAT MADRID RAG

By JULIUS LENZBERG

166   *That Madrid Rag*

"That's-A-Plenty."

(Rag Or One Step.)

by Lew Pollack

Allegro moderato.

TRIO.

Toots

Rag One Step

for Piano

by

Felix Arndt

116234 - 10 CELLO & PIANO
Price 50¢ net

116229 - PIANO SOLO
Price 60¢

G. Ricordi & Co

14 EAST 43 RD STREET
NEW YORK

AND AT LONDON, PARIS, LEIPSIG, ROME, PALERMO
NAPLES, BUENOS-AYRES AND MILAN.

TOOTS
A Rag One Step

FELIX ARNDT

173

TRIO

TOWN TALK

A CLASSIC IN RAGTIME
BY ELMER OLSON

BICKHART'S SONG SHOP
· MINNEAPOLIS · MINN ·

⑥

FEATURED BY
HIRSCHEL HENDLER
THE POET *of the* PIANO
OVER THE
ORPHEUM CIRCUIT

TOWN TALK
A Classic in Rag Time

by ELMER OLSON

Whipped Cream

Rag

FEATURE NUMBER BEING USED
by
EVELYN NESBIT
and
JACK CLIFFORD

by

PERCY WENRICH

5

Whipped Cream.
A Rag.

Introduction.

by Percy Wenrich.

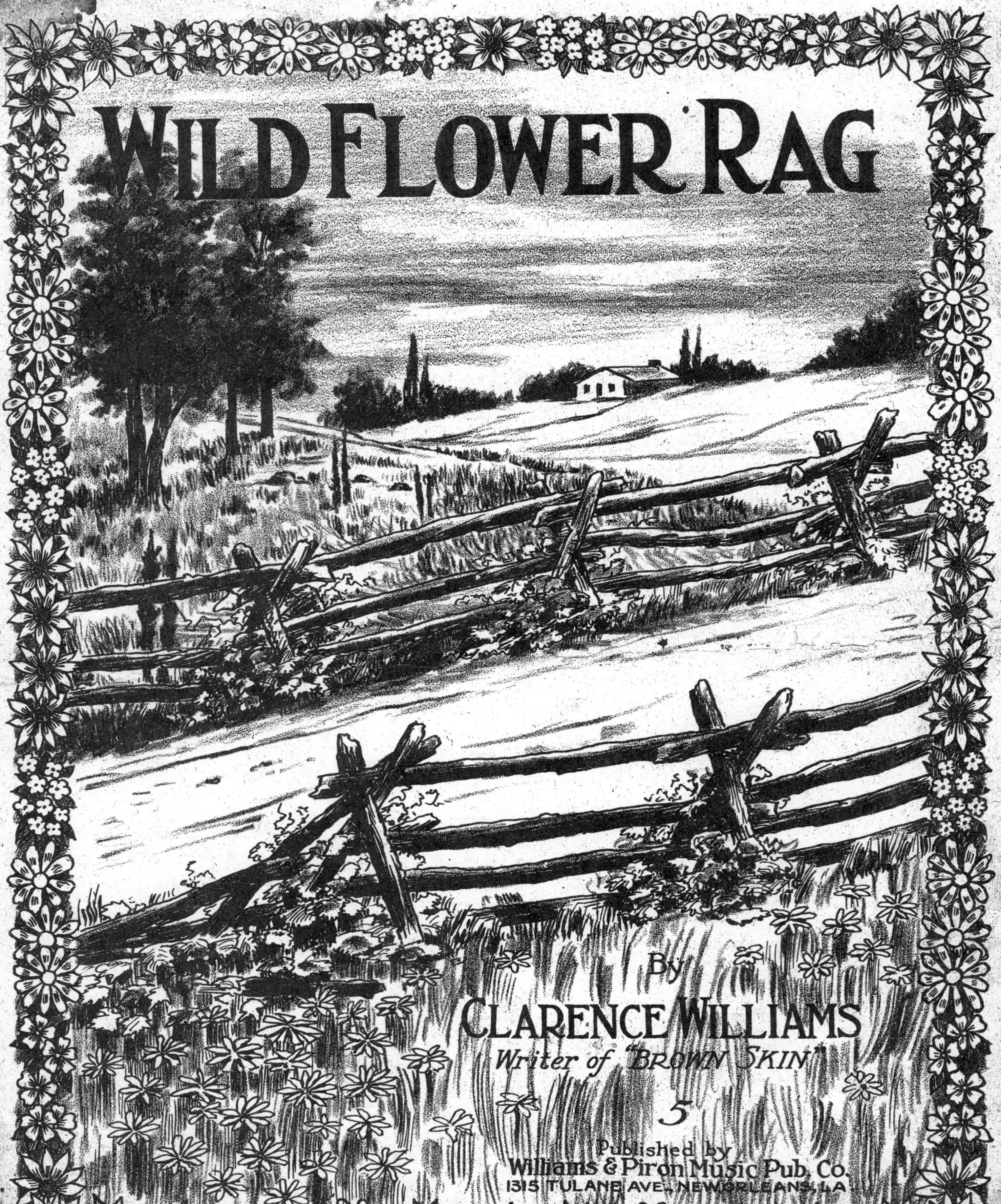
WILD FLOWER RAG
By
CLARENCE WILLIAMS
Writer of "BROWN SKIN"
5
Published by
Williams & Piron Music Pub. Co.
1315 TULANE AVE., NEW ORLEANS, LA.

Dedicated to Loius Wade and Fred C. Washington

WILD FLOWER RAG

By CLARENCE WILLIAMS

END OF EDITION